DADDY's Girl Forever

*Come Home to the Truth
About God's Heart Towards
You*

VANESSA A. HARRIS

DADDY's Girl Forever
COPYRIGHT © 2016 Vanessa A. Harris.

Unless otherwise noted, all Scripture quotations are taken from the New King James Version of the Bible. Copyright © 1982 by Thomas Nelson, Inc. Used by permission. All rights reserved.

Scripture quotations marked NLT are taken from the Holy Bible, New Living Translation copyright© 1996, 2004, 2007, 2013 by Tyndale House Foundation. Used by permission of Tyndale House Publishers Inc., Carol Stream, Illinois 60188. All rights reserved.

Scripture quotations marked NIV are taken from the Holy Bible, New International Version. Copyright © 1973, 1978, 1984 by Biblica, Inc. All rights reserved worldwide. (New International Version Bible Online)

Scripture quotations marked AMP are taken from the Amplified Bible. Copyright © 1954, 1958, 1962, 1964, 1965, 1987 by The Lockman Foundation. Used by permission. (www.lockman.org)

Scripture taken from The Message. Copyright © 1993, 1994, 1995, 1996, 2000, 2001, 2002. Used by permission of NavPress Publishing Group.

Some names and identifying details have been changed to protect the privacy of individuals.

Cover design by Cover Design Studio
Editing by Marja Humphrey, Ph.D.

Printed in the United States of America
First printing, 2016
ISBN 978-0-9972923-0-5

www.vinelifefaith.com

To my sweet
Little angel.

M Rayo and

GayleRayo.

To Hannah

Contents

Can We Talk...

When you think of your relationship with God the Father, what image comes to mind? Is it the furrowed brow and crossed arms of a fault-finder, barking intimidating demands? Is it the smile and affection of a Father whose love is the basis of His every interaction with you? Or is it an unpredictable hybrid of both?

Your relationship with your father influences your relationship with God the Father, either fostering or hindering a good opinion of Him. The truth is, God's not cold and distant. He doesn't relate to you based on your performance or your experience with your father. He doesn't have a laundry list of expectations and He's not difficult to please. God is good, and He wants you to enjoy His goodness.

To those of us made children of God through faith in Jesus Christ, He's our DADDY God, Abba. It's the very name Jesus called Him, denoting their intimate Father-Son relationship.[1] As wonderful a relationship as some of us enjoy with our fathers, it is only a foretaste of the dynamic we're meant to enjoy with our DADDY God.

Others of us who've suffered the rejection or loss of our fathers need to know we're not abandoned and hopeless. Our DADDY God draws us close. Those of us who've had tumultuous relationships with our fathers may fear our wrongs disqualify us from a loving father-daughter relationship with God. Know this: there is NOTHING that can separate you from the love of God in Christ Jesus our Lord (Romans 8:39)!

Girls **always** need their daddy, their DADDY God even more so. The void left by the absence of the first

2

creates a chasm between us and DADDY God that may seem impossible to cross. It's not! DADDY God provided His Son, Jesus, on a cross to bridge the gap. This revelation is crucial, since without it we turn to other means to establish our value.

Some throw themselves into unhealthy relationships with men, the topic of many a talk show. Others self-protect, keeping relationships at a safe distance, preferring instead to depend on our own efforts or approval from others to find value and security. It is the survival mode of those of us believing we're abandoned.

We burden ourselves to be all things to all people and to make it look effortless. Lumping God into the mix as well, we think He's our toughest customer, our toughest critic. Therefore, we define our worth by how confident and capable we appear; our insecurities and weariness hidden behind a mask.

DADDY God wants to speak to the little girl in you. The one who knows she doesn't have it altogether, whose vulnerability is inescapable, and cries out for DADDY's reassurance and protection. The little girl who needs to know her DADDY loves her unconditionally, in spite of her mistakes and weaknesses. No matter our age or accomplishments, every girl needs her DADDY!

If you find it hard to believe DADDY God's heart of love for you, you are not alone. Between the mischaracterizations I've heard preached about Him and my own relationship with my father, it's taken longer than I'd like to replace the false tape that's played in my mind for years. The more I meditate on Scripture verses affirming DADDY God's unconditional love for me and fill my ears with sermon messages on His grace, the more I believe the best about Him and His heart toward me.

That's why this book exists, to counter wrong beliefs about DADDY God that rob us girls of the fulfilling life He has for us. For years, as a believer, I struggled with anger and resentment toward God, but He never took offense and never let go of me. Instead, He pursued me with the truth of His goodness, winning me over.

In this book, I've also included glimpses into the lives of DADDY's girls I've known for years. These courageous women share their struggles stemming

4

from their relationships with their fathers and how their relationship with DADDY God causes them to triumph. This is the DADDY God I hope to share with you. I believe, as we talk, you'll draw nearer to Him as you discover more about DADDY's perfect love for you.

"...the sweet echo of those footsteps

returning."

ONE

Come Home

She wrinkles her nose, wiping the tip off the counter. A $1.27. Not gonna go very far in keeping her lights on, but something's better than nothing. The manager's voice interrupts her musings rattling on about Thanksgiving plans with family tomorrow. It's the first year the restaurant will close for it, and <u>almost</u> every one's excited. Picturing her empty fridge, she's too broke to even manage a sigh. She'd rather work. At least she would have gotten a good meal out of the deal.

When asked about her plans, she doesn't answer. Instead she glances around the dining room filled with smiles and laughter. She remembers her mom's smile and good cooking, the faces around the table, and her biting words to her dad. It was the last they spoke and she went too far. She wonders if Daddy would mind her stopping by for a little while...

As she rounds the corner by the old bodega, the wind whips through her thin coat. Seems like forever since she walked these familiar streets, but it's only been 2 years. Waves of childhood memories wash over her with every step. Daddy is a good man and overall, he's been good to her. She rounds the corner, two blocks to go. Rehearsing new words for her father, she presses on.

Meanwhile her father pulls into the driveway with last minute groceries. Opening the trunk, he catches himself expecting to see the nosy girl who could never resist a shopping bag. Despite her absence, his lips curl at the memory. While gathering the bags and his senses, he hears gentle footsteps stop behind him. He knows who they belong to and how long he waited to hear them again. As he turns wet-faced, words spill out of her mouth, without the venom of their last meeting.

He doesn't even hear them. All he hears is the sweet echo of those footsteps returning. All he sees is his beautiful little girl. All he does is kiss and hold her, escorting her inside, then seating her at the table. This is where she belongs. His daughter is near again, so it's time to celebrate. There's so much to be thankful for!

• • •

How many of us would love that kind of reunion with our fathers instead of the furrowed brows of disappointment, the frozen shoulder of rejection, or the silence of his absence? Some may have had a major falling out with their fathers; others of us have experienced a slow distancing over time. Maybe you've always felt distant from your father, and the chasm seems too wide to bridge. It's painful, I understand. Here's the reality. No matter your relationship with your father, that woman you just read about; the one welcomed home, *is* you. She's me too.

The anticipation and delight of the father portrayed above only hints at the utter joy DADDY God has when His daughters believe He's good, and return to Him. The vignette is based on Jesus' parable of "The Prodigal Son" found in Luke 15. Most times I've heard someone preach or teach the parable, they emphasized the younger son's rebelliousness. They spoke of him as if a young stallion needing to be broken. Pastor Joseph Prince is the first person I ever heard preaching what Jesus emphasized in the parable—the love of the father typifying the love of *His* Father, DADDY God! Since then, the more I study the parable, the more the Holy Spirit reveals the magnitude of my DADDY God's love.

The parable highlights a common misconception among believers and DADDY God's response to it. If you're unfamiliar with the account, please indulge me. The father has two sons, the younger of which demands what he thinks he deserves --- his share of the inheritance, though his father is alive and kicking! He takes the money and blows it partying. Broke as a joke with no punch line, now in a famine ravaged land, he aligns himself with a man who sends him to work feeding pigs! Unless you're a pig farmer I can't imagine a more horrible lot, but it's especially so for a Jew.

The job doesn't even pay well enough. Though working, he's starving, yet his employer won't give him anything to eat. Tempted to eat pig slop, he remembers how well his father's servants eat. He concludes that worthy son or not, his father would gladly feed him if he demotes himself to a servant. Pure hunger drives him home and to craft a speech he believes will be music to his father's ears, "I'm no longer worthy to be your son."

The son comes home thinking he simply needs his belly filled; he doesn't realize he needs his heart filled with his father's love. The father knows it. When he sees his son in the distance he has compassion. The Greek word used for compassion is used throughout the gospels, usually with regard to Jesus. Always moved by needs, He quickly met them without considering the person's merit.

In this parable the father is touched by his son's need for love and grace. He takes off running to meet him. Now, the son knows he messed up. It's undeniable; he's unkempt and reeks like a pig. The last thing he expects is an affectionate welcome, but in actuality, he **needs to know** his father loves him. His father always loved him. The son never did anything to deserve his father's love and his current state doesn't disqualify him now. It's one thing when someone tells you they love you while you're doing right, but you know it's true when they hug and kiss you in your wretchedness. I'm pretty sure some mother just said, "AMEN," right there!

Still, true to character, the young man starts running his mouth. His father's kisses still wet on his cheek, arms wrapped around him; the son begins his prepared speech. The father immediately interrupts to meet the second need...grace. Grace, by the way, means undeserved, unmerited favor or kindness.[1] It *is* what the Gospel is all about. God so loved the world that He gave His only begotten Son and with His Son came grace and truth (see John 3:16, John 1:17). Jesus is the manifested grace of God. Just as we don't deserve Jesus, the last thing this son *deserves* is his father's best robe, ring and shoes, after all the harsh words and horrible waste. Yet that's exactly what his father gives him and tells the servants to prepare for a no holds barred party!

What is going on you ask? Is this father insane? Not at all! He relishes the opportunity to show his love and grace can *never* be earned and is only enjoyed by those who know they don't deserve it. Now that fellowship is restored, his son will eventually realize believing he had to earn his father's love only made him bitter, reckless. He'll remember that at his worst, his father lavished him with love and blessed him beyond his wildest dreams.

It's the truth Jesus wants you and me to believe about His Father. No matter where you've been or what you've done, and yes, even as a believer, your DADDY God loves you and longs for you. Don't stay away fearing His anger, believing you let Him down. If you've put your faith in Jesus' work at the cross, you've already been completely forgiven. Your faith in Jesus Christ justified you forever; in DADDY God's eyes it's "just as if you never sinned." Since Christ made you right with DADDY God, you can enjoy peace with Him. In fact, He is so satisfied with Jesus' work, He promises "your sins and lawless deeds He'll remember no more (Hebrews 8:12)."

> "Oh, what joy for those whose disobedience is forgiven, whose sins are put out of sight. Yes, what joy for those whose record the LORD has cleared of sin."
> — Romans 4:7-8, NLT

Toss the idea your DADDY God is constantly mulling over your mistakes. He doesn't think about them because He's already punished Jesus for them in your place. Nothing, including sin, can separate you from DADDY God's love (see Romans 8:39). Come home to the outpouring of His love and grace.

DADDY God invites you to come get to know the love, joy, and security found only in His arms! He anticipates your arrival, His heart longing to hear the sweet echo of your footsteps returning. Will you come home?

TWO

Fathers and Daughters

What kind of relationship did you have with your father growing up? Did you spend quality time with him? Did you feel secure in his love? Did he give you the sense you were enough, just as you were? What is your relationship like today?

I grew up in a two-parent household the daughter of West Indian immigrants, both of them hard-working. Without hesitation, I'd say, I was a daddy's girl as a child. It's no surprise really. I spent so much time with my dad because my mom worked nights as far back as I can remember. In many ways I'm a lot like him, and as a young girl I felt very much like his little princess.

The dynamic started changing during elementary school. Everything became performance focused, less about our relationship. My father became increasingly hard to please academically, with warm cuddles eventually replaced with quick hugs. You can imagine how devastating that was for a girl who'd previously and effortlessly felt like her daddy's delight.

On my end, I've always been my dad's biggest fan. The stories he and my uncles told about growing up on their tiny island nation are some of my favorite memories. To this day, my dad is my biggest inspiration. There is no quit in him despite the odds he faced so young.

That's probably why the growing distance hit me so hard. Yes, we lived in the same home, but we weren't close anymore. We've always communicated, but it's become increasingly awkward and I don't know why. Maybe it was because I wasn't a boy. My father mentioned here and there he preferred boys over girls because "they didn't bring trouble home." I was an 'A' student, though, and didn't "cause trouble."

Maybe he distanced himself because of his and my older sister's severely strained relationship that completely derailed in her teens. Could he merely have been bracing himself for the worse by slowly shutting me out too? Maybe he felt I'd become a big girl, past the age of needing his affection and affirmation?

When I was about 15, my mom said something that cut me to the quick and left me hemorrhaging for years. "Your dad didn't want you." She went on to say that since my dad already had children from his first marriage, he didn't want any more with her. She said she had to beg him to have a child with her and, he hoped I'd be a boy. If that's so, he didn't get what he wanted...

There's also the impact growing up without his father had on him. Could it have been a combination of all of them; a perfect storm that left me shipwrecked? All these unanswered questions left me insecure, no longer sure my dad wanted me, much less loved me. I wanted my dad to enjoy me again, but I didn't know how to make it happen and I never figured out how.

Well over a decade ago, the Lord led my husband and me to a difficult decision. I would stay home to raise our children after I completed my second residency. Recently, during our homeschooling years, my father called to tell me both he and my mother were "so very disappointed in me" for not working as a physician. In effect, honoring my DADDY meant disappointing my dad. That hurt me in a way only a loved one can!

To be fair, I know my parents love me the best they've known love. They worked hard to set me up for as much success as I could dare dream of. That's a blessing for which I am eternally grateful. As for my relationship with my dad, I love him, despite the distance and hurtful words between us. He's a great man and I'm proud to be his daughter!

Unknowingly, though, his rejection over the years took a toll on me. As much as I loved and needed my dad, he seemed displeased with me despite my achievements. Our interactions became formal and dutiful, rather than genuine and loving. Looking back, I see how that impacted me in other areas. I started anticipating rejection at every turn. Anger began lurking beneath the surface, manifesting as depression.

For years I struggled with bouts of deep depression that seemed to swallow me whole. Subconsciously I saw myself as a reject, desperately needing to prove I wasn't. The perfectionist monster emerged! I needed outcomes to be as perfect as possible to feel safe and prove my life worthwhile.

Maybe you read this and say,

"So what, at least you knew your father. I've never met mine."

"My father's been locked away in prison since I was a little girl."

"My father up and left, and never looked back."

"My father passed away and I'll never see him again."

There's no prize for having the worst story. Whatever the story, the pain is real and the effects can last into womanhood. Regina's story is different to mine with a completely different family dynamic.

Her parents conceived her as a very young, unmarried couple and try as she might she never could get close to her father. She gave up hope around age 7 after overhearing her father questioning her paternity. After losing her mother as a teenager, hoped revived; her father promising to be present in her life. Maybe now she and her father could build a relationship after all those years? Sadly, it didn't play out that way. Today she is left with the memory of a promise unfulfilled and no desire for a relationship with him.

Isn't it interesting that when she thought she gave up hope, she really hadn't? Years later when her father promised to be there for her as the only surviving parent, there was hope waking from slumber. While she eventually discarded hope in her father, she's thankful she found faithfulness in DADDY God and her savior, Jesus Christ. Do you think Regina found it easy to believe God loved her and would care for her as a Father? Probably not, the word 'father' had become associated with rejection and empty promises. None the less, the longer she walks with her DADDY God, the more she trusts Him.

I don't think it's a stretch to say our relationship with our father greatly impacts our perspective of the heavenly One. If we can't trust the heart of the father we can see, it's harder to trust the heart of the Father we can't. Jesus, Himself, acknowledges He is the only one who's seen the Father (see John 6:46), but says in seeing Him, you've seen the Father (see John 14:9). Jesus is the only man who perfectly represents the Father.

However, for those who enjoy a father's loving, affirming, and protective presence, it's easier to believe God the Father does likewise. On the other hand, those who experienced a father's rejection through absence, silence or harsh words, may feel insecure in their relationship with God the Father. They may expect Him to lose interest or leave them when they fall short, if they receive Him as Father at all. Some of us, like Sheila, know what it's like to be a dethroned "daddy's girl."

In a way, she considers herself a daddy's girl because she knew her alcoholic Vietnam Veteran father "loved her beyond measure," though his issues often got in the way. Hard days of manual labor culminated with trips to the liquor store and arguments, sometimes violent, with her mother. Once her mom, the family's anchor, passed away at a young age, Sheila and her brother were separated and sent to live with other family members in hopes of having more stability. Her family unit never got restored and, ultimately, she "became fiercely independent vowing to not have to rely on other people for [her] sense of stability."

I believe DADDY God wants Sheila to know He is fully invested in her well-being. She's not meant to tough it out alone. He is for her AND with her (see Isaiah 41:10). He is **for** every one of His girls. He is

for **you** and His plans for you are awesome. He didn't
save you to abandon to you. The cross declares He is
devoted to you, now and forever.

> "For I know the plans I have for
> you," declares the LORD, "plans to
> prosper you and not to harm you,
> plans to give you hope and a
> future." — Jeremiah 29:11, NIV

Believing the truth about our DADDY God's heart
is crucial to developing the healthy relationship with
Him Jesus sacrificed to give us, regardless of our
relationship with our fathers. I want to tell you
something that, if you believe it in your heart, will
transform your life. **There is no direct correlation
between our fathers' thoughts, attitudes, and behavior
toward us and DADDY God's heart for us, period.**
Ideally, yes, our fathers would provide a tangible
glimpse of our potential relationship with DADDY
God. Some beautifully reflect His heart as humanly
possible, though imperfectly, and some miss the mark
horribly.

We can't see them and DADDY God as one and the same because no man, other than Jesus, can truly convey DADDY God's love for us. He alone loves perfectly and unconditionally. He sacrificed His best for our good, at great cost. He cannot lie and He keeps every promise (see Numbers 23:19). This is the heart of our DADDY God!

Let's face it. All of us girls are on equal ground. We were all born with the same longing to be accepted, secure, delighted in, and cherished. No matter our relationships with our fathers, DADDY God is more than able to satisfy our longing souls.

> When my mother and my father
> forsake me, then the LORD will
> take me up. — Psalm 27:10, KJV

This is DADDY God's answer to the aching soul. By the time I came across this promise I'd already felt forsaken (rejected). Though somewhat comforting, just knowing these words didn't soothe the pain. Years later I began meditating on that verse, word for word, asking the Holy Spirit to make it real to me.

Soon after, He answered me during a Joseph Prince Ministries broadcast when Pastor Prince said, "Like the children of Israel then, believers today ask God to remove the source of our problem when, instead, God's solution is to give us a revelation of the cross of Christ." In the past, I just wanted God to fix it; either restore the relationship or take away the pain of what it had become. Neither was best because pain so deep must be dealt with. It's the revelation of the cross that deals with the source and its effects. So...I asked the Holy Spirit to show me how Jesus dealt with my rejection on the cross.

He told me to look up, in a sense, and reminded me of some of Jesus' last words on the cross. Do you remember them? "My God, My God, why have You forsaken Me (Mark 15:34)?" You see, on the cross Jesus took my place as the abandoned. There He hung, His Father having turned His back on Him. Did Jesus deserve it? No. He was abandoned because He bore my sin, yours and all mankind, but He was abandoned none the less.

He experienced His DADDY turning away from Him, so DADDY could turn to *me*. My sin dealt with,

DADDY God accepted and received me (the meaning of the Hebrew word for "take me up" in Psalm 27).[1] He abandoned Jesus, so He could welcome me home (and all who believe in Jesus). DADDY God *wanted* me. He even pursued me to be a father to me. Thanks to Jesus I have a DADDY who thoroughly accepts me and even temporarily turned His back on His Perfect Son to do it!

> For God so loved the world that
> He gave His only begotten Son,
> that whoever believes in Him
> should not perish but have
> everlasting life. — John 3:16

Can you imagine the conversation that brought this plan about? Please indulge my imagination for a moment.

• • •

Knowing all things for all eternity, Father, Son and Holy Spirit sit around a table watching the events of the yet unformed world unfold before them. They watch the people they would make, suffering in the condemned flesh passed down by the one who ate from the fateful tree.

"We made them for fellowship, but look how they're destroying themselves, helpless to stop. I love them and I want to be close to them again," says the Father.

The Son eyes His Father and replies, "We already know what must be done, Father, and I'm ready to go."

"Son, this is no small thing, as You know. You will suffer the indignity of bearing the likeness of human flesh, including their sicknesses and sorrows. You'll carry the weight of sin for all mankind and die the death of a common criminal in their place after enduring my punishing wrath."

"Yes, Father, I have counted the cost and it is great, but I love them as much as you do. The opportunity to bring them home is worth it."

The Holy Spirit consents by adding, "Most Holy God, I know Your Son is precious to You. I stand ready at Your Word, to work for and through Him to both bring this to pass and bring glory to His name."

· · ·

Jesus says, speaking of Himself, "There is no greater love than to lay down one's life for one's friends (John 15:13, NLT)." There's no denying that, but what about the love of the Father who offered Jesus to be sacrificed? He didn't have to. He could have abandoned humanity to our hopeless fate, but He didn't. I'd say His love is just as great. Friend, what do you say?

THREE

DADDY's Girl Forever

Your father may have walked away from you physically or emotionally, but the Holy Spirit wants you to know DADDY God pursues you. He desires to be all you need Him to be. That image you may have of God always turning away from you is a lie!

He is always moving toward you, calling you to Him. It's amazing to think about DADDY God pursuing us in our hopeless sin state by sending His Son. Now that Jesus has paid for <u>and</u> put away believers' sin forever, there is nothing that could ever cause DADDY God to reject us.

I'll tell you what's real to me today. The day I received Christ as Savior, I became a DADDY's girl again. It's true no matter how long it takes to sink in! The Holy Spirit continues to draw me near with unveilings of DADDY God's tender heart towards me (see John 16:13). I'm so thankful the Holy Spirit doesn't mind repeating Himself!

A couple years ago, I woke up and looked toward the ceiling, smiling a 'good morning' to DADDY God. Still in a sleepy haze I heard His inward voice say, "I saw everything that happened to you as a child. It hurt Me as much as it hurt you, but I knew I would restore you." My eyes widened immediately and filled with tears. A loving, warm sensation radiated throughout my body. What an unexpected and awesome statement greeting me first thing in the morning!

You know what really got me? He said, "everything;" it meant He doesn't miss a moment of my life, and I felt so loved and cared for. DADDY God drew near to me to let me know He does see, He didn't forget me, and He takes care of His own!

He didn't tell me that so I could just feel warm and tingly all over. He told me that to challenge what I'd believed about Him. My DADDY God wasn't a distant and casual observer of my life. He saw the heartache and the injustices and had already provided the answer. Now He needed to connect the dots to help me see it.

> And we know that all things work
> together for good to those who
> love God, to those who are the
> called according to His purpose.
> — Romans 8:28

This is one of the first verses I memorized and is one of my favorites. I'm the first to admit I've had a hard time recognizing it at work in the painful situations of life. It's just not a perspective that comes easily to me and I have always needed the Holy Spirit to reveal it. While many say "what doesn't kill you makes you stronger," I find what doesn't kill you can often make you bitter and I'd become bitter toward my dad. Once I acknowledged the bitterness and told DADDY God I had enough, the Holy Spirit began showing me the good that's come from our dynamic.

My dad keeping me emotionally at arm's length and hungry for unconditional love wounded me, and the devil meant for it to destroy me, but ultimately God used it to bless me. It actually set me up for a new life in Christ at age 19 and the loving relationship with my DADDY God I enjoy today. Jesus Christ is DADDY God's answer to the question: "Is there any such thing as a father's love without limit or qualification?" Yes! <u>Jesus Christ on the cross is the embodiment of God's pure and unconditional love!</u>

> I pray that out of his glorious riches he may strengthen you with power through his Spirit in your inner being, so that Christ may dwell in your hearts through faith. And I pray that you, being rooted and established in love, may have power, together with all

the saints, to grasp how wide and
long and high and deep is the love
of Christ, and to know this love
that surpasses knowledge—that
you may be filled to the measure
of all the fullness of God. —
Ephesians 3: 16-19, NIV

Sure, my dad "pushed me out of his lap," but he
ultimately pushed me onto DADDY God's! It HAS
been worked out for my good. Our relationship, such
as it is, has great purpose. It helped drive me to the
feet of Jesus and keeps me in DADDY God's face to
this very day.

I can let my dad off the emotional hook. So what
visiting with me and my family isn't a priority for him,
nor are speaking words of acceptance over me. I have
a DADDY with me at all times whose favor surrounds
me as with a shield (Psalm 5:12). My chats with my
DADDY God are completely transformational. He
patiently guides me, never frustrated by slow learning
curves. He believes the best about me, encouraging

me to see myself as He does. Most of all, He assures me that I'm deeply loved.

For too long I've been hung up on missing the physical expressions of love from my dad (i.e. visits, hugs, and approving smiles) when for more than 20 years my DADDY God's been smiling over me, encouraging, and loving me. Not to mention these last few years of *allowing* Christ to feed, strengthen and restore me, as the Holy Spirit convicts me of my righteousness in Him (see Psalm 23:1-3, John 16:7-11)! I'm surrounded by God's affirming presence. I've got a good thing going!

My dad and I don't owe each other anything. I forgive his shortcomings as I hope my children forgive mine. I choose to stop holding myself hostage to bitterness waiting for him to give me what he can't or won't. I accept him as he is and the reality of our relationship, without letting it define me anymore. That's the only way I'm free to enjoy my DADDY God, who satisfies my mouth with good things (Psalm 103:5), removing every trace of its bitterness.

In this verse, the Hebrew words translated 'satisfies' and 'mouth' would typically convey fulfilling one's desire to please God with fine outward adornment. Since the psalm is referring to God's actions, it is God who makes us pleasing to Him and He does it through His Son's, finished work. In this case God **tells** us He's satisfied with us, so our desire to please Him is satisfied!

The first time the word bitter is used in Scripture it describes Esau's cry to his father. Esau and Jacob were twins born to Isaac and Rebecca. With their mother's help Jacob deceived Isaac and stole the priceless firstborn blessing belonging to Esau, as the older twin (see Genesis 25 and 27). When Esau found out he was devastated, knowing the magnitude of his loss. Then he bitterly cried out for his father to bless him in some way. Any blessing was better than none at all. In those days a father's spoken blessing was everything; the trajectory of your life depended on the quality of that blessing.

It's no different for you and me today. If your father can't or won't bless you with his words, then who better to receive it from than DADDY God! If your father totally abandoned you, turn to your DADDY God in total abandon. What you need is the blessing; don't get hung up on who won't give it to you.

Don't get me wrong, a father's blessing is great to have, but his isn't the ultimate. Even though Jacob had his father, Isaac's, blessing, it wasn't until Jacob wrestled with God that he received his identity and purpose. God renamed him from Jacob, a trickster, to Israel, a prince of God (see Genesis 32:27-28, KJV). There's nothing like DADDY God's blessing!

It's amazing that reading God's Word and hearing sound preaching opens us up to the truth about DADDY God's heart towards us. I can't begin to tell you the blessing Joseph Prince's ministry has been to me and my family, though you've probably figured it out from the number of times I've mentioned him! There is one phrase of his that rings in my ear, "right believing leads to right living." It's not someone else's right beliefs that cause me to act right; it's what I believe (see Proverbs 23:7). It's me believing the truth about DADDY God and His heart towards me that completely transforms my life.

Our fathers may never give us daughters blanket acceptance. Does that mean that without it our lives hang in limbo or that we should forever doubt our value? That depends on how much weight we give their approval. If we base our value on receiving their acceptance, we will weary ourselves from waving our hands and pointing to our achievements trying to get them to notice us. That is nothing more than bondage, continuing the cycle of despair and defeat. Our fathers' approval is not a prize to be won. Christ is our approval, received simply through faith in Him. In Him, DADDY God is satisfied with us and I'm learning to be satisfied with my DADDY's satisfaction.

"That's all well and good," you may say, "but there's nothing like a hug from your dad when everything's going sideways to make you feel like everything is going to be alright." I hear you and I've felt the same way at times, but if that's not possible, what's the answer? Running into every available pair of arms you can find trying to find security? How's that worked for you? Though not tangible, your DADDY God is able to comfort you with His presence, as Danielle discovered for herself.

At 8 months' pregnant, Danielle had a car accident that landed her in intensive care. After coming off life support, she felt like she had nothing to live for since her own father didn't want her. As her mother and brother continued to pray for her she recalls hearing God's voice telling her to fight to live. Later that night she woke from a medicated haze to find her father at her bedside! He'd been watching her sleep every night for the past week, even though they hadn't had contact with each other for quite some time. While happy to see him, she knew his presence was simply DADDY God's way of confirming His words of encouragement to her. He wanted her to know, no matter how far away He seems, He is always with her, protecting her.

Her story illustrates one of my favorite psalms.

> The LORD is your keeper; the
> LORD is your shade at your right
> hand. The sun shall not strike you
> by day, nor the moon by night.
> The LORD shall preserve you
> from all evil; He shall preserve
> your soul. The LORD shall
> preserve your going out and your
> coming in from this time forth,
> and even forevermore. — Psalm
> 121:5-8

By the time I highlighted these verses in my bible I was in medical school, well past 18, and legally no longer my father's responsibility. Contrary to public perceptions of Bronxites, this girl from the Bronx had become insecure because I felt exposed. The journey to medical school had been an uphill battle, my wounded pride proof enough. Everyone in medical school is smart, but now battle weary, I didn't know if I could see my dream through to the end.

Does a woman ever outgrow her father's attentiveness and its insulating comfort, or does she just compensate by becoming overly suspicious, putting up walls, and frequently glancing over her shoulders? For me and many other women I've met, it appears to be the latter.

When I homeschooled my children, I taught my sons a science lesson on the characteristics of planets in our solar system. Those with no or thin atmospheres are more susceptible to wild temperature swings and collisions with meteors. Atmosphere has an insulating affect, that when absent or insufficient renders planets vulnerable and ultimately unwelcoming. Fathers have a similar effect. They serve as atmosphere for daughters and sons alike.

Their presence provides shelter from life's harsh extremes, especially for their daughters. His involvement in his daughter's life gives her resilience in the face of challenges, while allowing her to be vulnerable in his presence. There's a tenderness that's lost when a female feels uncovered at any age. I'm not talking about singleness or living on your own. I'm referring to the sense that you're doing life in the raw. No voice of wise counsel, no one to bounce ideas off of, and no one with ready words of encouragement when life kicks you in the rear.

I developed a toughness because I felt unprotected and alone. It had nothing to do with weakness. Growing up in the Bronx, I'd seen and experienced things that would give some pause. Back in those days, my confidence and perseverance directly correlated with my connection to my dad. When I was *his* girl I felt safe; his presence reassured me.

Remember Danielle, who unexpectedly saw her dad at her bedside after her accident? She's appreciative of her childhood relationship with her dad because he "taught [her] how to interact with people without fear, only confidence. He also taught [her] how to find the good in every situation, which taught [her] resilience." She reflects on these memories without pain because now she's confident in DADDY God's love for her. So much so, she and her father have re-established a loving relationship. He even calls Danielle, "his little girl," every chance he gets. Though now an adult, Danielle never tires of hearing it! That's the restoring power of God's love, the soul first, then the relationships.

I don't think we outgrow the need to be "his" girl, but we need to make the shift to His girl. Those verses in Psalm 121 promised the security I didn't know I still needed. At that time, I didn't have a revelation of my DADDY God's complete acceptance of me. I didn't know I was His girl, so our relationship still felt as distant and formal as mine and my father's. I interpreted the psalm's promised protection as one based on duty rather than love, requiring me to meet certain expectations in return.

It didn't help that I heard God characterized that way from the pulpit most of my life. The impression given, "He loves you so much He sent His Only Son to die in your place; now get your act together and don't make Him regret it." It sounds ridiculous even now as I write it. How in the world could you feel secure in God's hands under those conditions? Yet many of us fed on some variation of that in the Church for years. Many still do. In reality He lovingly **gives without demanding** anything in return.

He offered me more than His Son, He offered to hold my hand as I walk alongside Him, but I didn't believe Him. My hands were fisted, ready to fight anyone who would take advantage of me. The posture of a woman left alone to navigate an unforgiving, unkind world.

That morning He told me He would restore me; He invited me to look away from what I'd experienced, to trust Him. Trust that He's not a supersized version of my dad; in fact, He's unlike any one I've met, heard of, or imagined. He had hold of me, my security no longer a question, but did I believe it? Would I uncurl my fingers to take *His* "hand?"

That's another story because that meant risk. What would I do if God kept me at arm's length, only helping with the "heavy lifting," but never lifting the veil over His heart? What if I did something that ruined our relationship; my princess coach suddenly turned back into the pumpkin I sit on while stranded by the road side? How would I cope if He became displeased and turned His back on me?

Have you ever asked these questions? The good news is there is no veil, no thing that could ever separate us from our DADDY's love (see Romans 8:39). Let's uncurl those fingers and embrace His love! Remember, your DADDY God is not well-meaning, but unreliable. He is Almighty God and His promises are sure (see Genesis 17:1, 2 Corinthians 1:20)! As for turning away from us...

> ...for He [God] Himself has said, I will not in any way fail you nor give you up nor leave you without support. [I will] not, [I will] not, [I will] not in any degree leave you helpless nor forsake nor let [you] down (relax My hold on you)! [Assuredly not!]
> — Hebrews 13:5, AMP

I love how the amplified version conveys God's blatant sincerity. He's not going anywhere. He's too busy enjoying what Christ's done for us!

> The LORD your God is with you, the Mighty Warrior who saves. He will take great delight in you; in his love he will no longer rebuke

you, but will rejoice over you with

singing." — Zephaniah 3:17, NIV

I can't get enough of those words. Can you? Read them over and over, savoring the meaning of each of them. What do you envision as you read those words? Do you *sense* the joy, the tenderness, and how He relishes you? This is the language of a Father cherishing His child, but to understand what made this possible, we have to go back to verse 15. That's where Zephaniah prophesies that Jesus will take the punishment we deserve.

What Zephaniah prophesied, we can enjoy today. Jesus fulfilled the prophecy at the cross by paying for and removing every displeasing thing about you and me from before His Father's eyes! Now we can also call him DADDY and He can enjoy us fully.

Our DADDY's love cannot be earned, only received; the very thing that quiets my anxious soul. His promised presence and unconditional love give me courage and boldness, yet quiets my brashness. Whenever I feel insecure about His love for me, He pursues me with fresh demonstrations of it!

His watching over and protecting His daughters has nothing to do with begrudging duty. He does it out of pure delight. Much in the way a mother silently watches her sleeping baby, enjoying the rise and fall of his breathing while dreaming of all she hopes for him. Our DADDY watches us day and night because we're precious to Him. He savors His love for each of us sandwiched between expressions of His joy and delight in the saving work of Jesus, the work that brought us back to Him. Oh He watches over us alright, not out of duty, but pure pleasure!

Your DADDY God loves you and delights in you to the point of breaking out in song. How exciting is that! In Christ, **you are a DADDY's girl, forever**. Your DADDY is near, faithful, and lovingly looks after you.

The most important man in your life may have rejected you, but your DADDY God sent another Man. In that Man, the Christ, you are always accepted. You bear your DADDY's name and He's pleased to call you His own. That's an awesome truth to let roll around your mind until it makes itself at home in your heart!

Calling All DADDY's Girls...

Are you a DADDY's girl? A DADDY's girl is a girl (of any age) who has received Jesus Christ as her Lord and Savior. Jesus is your hand delivered invitation from DADDY God; THE expression of His great love for you. There is no way to a relationship with God the Father except through His Beloved Son.

The good news is the hard part has already been done! Jesus went to the cross to pay the full cost for your entire life of sin. By believing Jesus completely paid for all that's wrong with you, you receive all that's right with Him and enjoy His perfect standing with DADDY God. It is a gift purely by grace; you cannot earn it or maintain it by your efforts. As generously as it is given, it must be wholeheartedly received. If you are ready to receive the gift of salvation in Jesus Christ, say from your heart,

"Heavenly Father, I am a sinner in desperate need of a Savior. I believe You sent Your Son, Jesus Christ, in the form of a man to pay the full price of my sin on the cross. Jesus Christ is Lord and I receive Him as my Savior. Since Jesus completely paid my debt, I am forgiven all forever. All that is left for me to do is rest in His perfect work and believe that Christ has made me right with You, DADDY God. I pray this in Jesus' name, Amen."

If you prayed that prayer, Jesus welcomes you to the family! DADDY God is rejoicing and the Holy Spirit now lives in you. Make yourself at home, my sister. You're a DADDY's girl forever!

FOUR

Nothing to Prove

Have you ever gotten that "look" when you walk in a room? The one with the question mark behind the eyes wondering, "Who are you and why should I care?" I have and it's usually from another woman. Do you know why I've *noticed* those looks? It's for the same reason they're *given*: insecurity caused by past rejection.

Remember in the last chapter I talked about how a father's rejection can trigger a self-protective response in his daughter? Well that insecurity also causes self-consciousness. You know when your thoughts are consumed with yourself and how you're perceived by others. Now you didn't think you were the only one with *that* hang up, did you?

Let's be honest. If you have no idea why the man who contributed half of his genes in your creation isn't interested in having a relationship with you, is it any wonder why, you might subconsciously expect to be discounted by random people for random reasons?

If you're an introvert, like me, that can make relating to others even more complicated. Like any "good" introvert, I tend to be introspective and self-analyzing, on my own accord and in reaction to others. Introverts also tend to enter rooms unassumingly. We smile, we're cordial, but we don't enter a room chatting everyone up looking to fit in. It's just not our style. If we come across a woman who has a history of experiencing rejection, our quiet demeanor is often misinterpreted by her as more rejection. That's so ironic since, by nature, introverts are quite considerate of others' feelings.

An introvert's flow is exactly opposite the "in your face" self-promotion that's become a societal norm.

We tend not to be open books, preferring instead to maintain a little mystery. It's actually fun for us to discover people over time instead of knowing their life story within five minutes of meeting them. It's neither right nor wrong; it's just a different perspective.

Unfortunately, the masses rarely appreciate unique perspectives and so introverts, among others branded 'different', often find ourselves recipients of the dreaded 'REJECT' stamp. Picture this: you're already rejected by your father for reasons unknown AND rejected by the world at large because you don't fit in "their box." What's a girl to do with all that?! Hold it up against the truth...

> Isn't it obvious that God deliberately chose men and women that the culture overlooks and exploits and abuses, chose these "nobodies" to expose the hollow pretensions of the "somebodies"? That makes it quite clear that none of you can get by

DADDY's Girl Forever
Come Home to the Truth About God's Heart Towards You

with blowing your own horn
before God.
—1 Corinthians 1:27-29, The
Message Bible

That tickles me! Turns out, God is drawn to the very ones most people find odd or have no use for! He loves doing things with, through, and for them that blows everyone else's minds. Some people just march to the beat of a different drum for any number of reasons, and not everyone catches on to their rhythm.

One day as I talked with the Lord about one of my son's quirky ways, the Holy Spirit broke it down for me like this, "What people call 'oddities' are the expressions of God's genius, confounding mankind." THAT was deep! After I closed my gaping mouth, I chuckled thinking about the number of people I've confounded, male and female alike!

Right then I knew I needed to cut that son of mine some slack and encourage him to embrace his quirky charm rather than view it negatively. It may mean fewer friends, but at least his friendships would be authentic. Whether you're introverted, quirky, or have some other personality trait that makes you stand out, rejection is a part of life. Just don't let it *define* your life. Instead, give the rejection to DADDY God and let Him show you the awe and wonder behind your design (see Psalm 139:14).

I've certainly experienced rejection in social circles, but I don't paint myself a victim of it. It makes me thankful for the friendships I've enjoyed all my life. For me there's nothing like true friends, rich in quality, though modest in quantity. I find friendships priceless and, like my money, I use the word 'friend' sparingly! You can imagine then, for me, sincere friendships take time to develop, but once you're "in," you're a friend for life. Can you blame me, really? I don't come by true friends easily!

On the flip side, this introvert has had her share of loneliness. People misinterpreting my words/actions and their superficial judgments are isolating in this unforgiving culture, leaving me no soft place to land. At every turn, at "home and abroad," I've felt expected to prove myself worthy of joining the group. So, in the name of self-preservation I often kept to myself. Limiting my interactions meant fewer people having expectations of me, fewer people to disappoint, and fewer people to reject me.   I'd had enough of that from my parents, so I dove deeper into my shell where I'd be "safe," but alone.

In my solitude, another issue emerged. I realized people's words followed me into the shell, staying with me long after their utterance, a subconscious gong echoing in my mind. Oh how much time I spent rehearsing a catty woman's dismissive words and actions, etching them into my memory! *Why did she look at me that way? Did I say something wrong? Why isn't she speaking to me all of a sudden? Why was I left out?* Why do we do that??! Why do we take someone's condemning words, own them as our own and then play them like a broken record?

If you're already introspective, even self-policing, and on top of that beat yourself up with someone else's words or perceptions, it's downright depressing. I can't tell you how many years I've wasted examining myself as if something's wrong with me. I wasn't more messed up than anyone else, but thanks to new life in Christ none of that matters! He is perfect and I'm hidden in that perfection (see Hebrews 5:9,

Colossians 3:3). Picking myself apart before someone else does it, is neither noble nor self-protective, it's foolish and self-destructive.

> We do not dare to classify or compare ourselves with some who commend themselves. When they measure themselves by themselves and compare themselves with themselves, they are not wise.
>
> — 2 Corinthians 10: 12, NIV

With all my second-guessing I became overly suspicious of people's motives, probably closing myself off from some potentially genuine friendships. Friendship is part of the abundant life Jesus came to give us and here I was denying myself (see John 10:10). Enough was enough; I had to risk (there goes that word again) in order to receive all He came to offer.

It took me a long time to realize experiencing rejection, no matter how often or by whom, didn't make me a reject. **My experience and my identity are**

not one in the same. I couldn't embrace that before discovering my DADDY's unconditional acceptance, founded on Jesus, who is eternal and far greater than me. Total security in Him allows me to risk possible rejection, in hopes of meeting other people who add dimension to my life, and vice versa.

If you are spending time trying to figure out why you're not fitting in, quit it! If you're in Christ, you found where you fit. Christ put His Spirit in you to make your unique attributes "pop" for His glory. You and I are not meant to identify with the masses. We should appreciate each other's unique qualities, but our identity is based on **who** we come from, rather than the people we associate with.

For many years I only identified with my family, my lineage, my heritage. I'm so proud of my lineage but I came *through* them, not *from* them. All of us came from the one true God created with great care (see Genesis 1:26). Handcrafted; our lives were designed and handwritten long before we breathed our first breath (see Psalm 139:15-16). Only when we receive Christ as Savior do we live out our true identity. Christ lives in us and we live by faith in who He is.

> I have been crucified with Christ;
> it is no longer I who live, but
> Christ lives in me; and the life
> which I now live in the flesh I live
> by faith in the Son of God, who
> loved me and gave Himself for me.
> — Galatians 2:20

In Christ we're the new creations Paul speaks of in 2 Corinthians. When we're born again, all the past ways we identified with and/or categorized ourselves are gone (see 2 Corinthians 5:17). The boxes that once contained us, now crushed and trashed. We are brand new! People may try to relate to us as if we're still in those boxes, but in our DADDY's eyes, we are new *and* flawless. All credit and glory to Christ Jesus for His perfect work on the cross, so highly regarded by DADDY God! Jesus' perfect and powerful blood accomplished what no other sacrifice could. DADDY God sees just as perfect, anyone who believes Jesus' powerful blood has cleansed them forever (see Hebrews 10:14). By DADDY God's grace we receive the favor Jesus deserves as well as the acceptance He enjoys as the Beloved.

> Blessed be the God and Father of our Lord Jesus Christ, who <u>has</u> <u>blessed us </u>with every spiritual blessing in the heavenly places in Christ, just as He chose us in Him before the foundation of the world, that we should be holy and without blame before Him in love, having predestined us to adoption as sons by Jesus Christ to Himself, according to the <u>good pleasure of</u> <u>His will</u>, to the praise of the glory of His grace, by which He made us <u>accepted in the Beloved</u>.
> —Ephesians 1:3-6, emphasis added

Ladies, in Christ, we are already blessed in every way imaginable! Did you notice it *pleased* DADDY

God to choose and adopt us in Jesus Christ, who sets us apart as faultless in DADDY God's eyes? And no, there's nothing wrong with God's eyes! He knows we mess up, but when He looks at His girls, He sees what He sees in Jesus—*pure perfection*. That ought to put a smile on your face and set your shoulders back!

When I walk into any environment these days, I'm much less concerned with people's perceptions. Who am I? I'm my DADDY's daughter and He enjoys me as I am, while His Spirit transforms me into all He made me to be. As long as He is for me, who can really be against me (see Romans 8:31)? I'm blessed to be a blessing (see Genesis 12:2) and I believe I'm a "blessing going somewhere to happen." Focused on Christ, and not myself, I can extend the grace I've received in abundance. It's all about what you believe and who you focus on.

> Summing it all up, friends, I'd say you'll do best by filling your minds and meditating on things true, noble, reputable, authentic, compelling, gracious - the best,

> not the worst; the beautiful, not
> the ugly; things to praise, not
> things to curse.
> —Philippians 4:8, The Message
> Bible

Do you know who ticks all the boxes in that verse? JESUS. These days I'm busy filling my mind with who Jesus is to me and who I am in Him. While I don't walk in a room expecting to be accepted by everyone, I don't walk in expecting rejection either. What I do expect is favor with whomever DADDY God gives me favor. The days of obsessing over my self-perception or how others esteem me are over! I'm so much more at ease in new social settings because I know I'm accepted and I don't have anything to prove.

Our DADDY God favors us because of what Jesus did on that cross. There He suffered rejection from His Father and mankind so that in Him we would have favor with God and people (see Luke 2:52). Favor with "man" does not mean favor with all people, because even Jesus had His share of haters. Yet, He didn't go around bracing Himself for confrontation or rejection.

Confident in His identity as God and the beloved Son of His Father, He went out anticipating being a blessing to those who saw Him that way.

That's so important for us and our children to remember in a world that's so quick to cast down and cast out based on what's superficial and temporary. DADDY God will lead you to the people who recognize His favor on you and the blessing He's made you. Feel free to ignore words to the contrary.

"There is no flaw in you!" — Song of Solomon 4:7b, AM

FIVE

Flawless!

Have you ever watched the pre-awards red carpet shows? I get a kick out of them. Sometimes I don't even stick around for the awards show, itself. Seeing who wears what and how well it is (or isn't) pulled together is so much more entertaining! The celebrities' goal, after all, is to put their best foot forward. Most rise to the occasion; others fall flat on their faces. When interviewed they're asked the most "pressing" question, "Who are you wearing?"

So, I ask you. "Who are you wearing?" Are you wearing the best fig leaves you could pull together, like Adam and Eve, trying to disguise your insecurities and weaknesses? How you see yourself directly correlates with how you think others see you. You can try to put on a show for others, but how you feel about yourself always surfaces.

Faking it is big business these days. Back in 2012, Forbes magazine wrote a piece on Sara Blakely and her billion dollar company, Spanx.[1] You and I and countless other women contributed our share to her pocket book, because of our obsession with appearing like everything is tight and right when it's really saggy and baggy. Cheers to Spanx, I do appreciate the brand! There are some outfits that ought not be worn without it! I'm all for looking good coming and going, but as Eve figured out, there isn't enough spandex in the world to fix the mess deep down inside.

When it comes to shortcomings, trying harder to drop those extra pounds of sin (our wrong habits, wrong thoughts, and wrong talk) or holding our stomachs in (pretense and self-denial) won't cut it. If sin was so easy to toss to the side, we wouldn't need a

Savior. Pretending you have it all together, when you don't, is pointless. We're all "sucking our stomachs in" one way or another! We may fool others temporarily, but we can't fool ourselves. We just end up feeling guiltier for being phony.

The truth is, on our best day, our self-improvement efforts are about as impressive as a soiled sanitary napkin! Yeah I said it but they're not my words, take it up with the prophet Isaiah. "But we are all like an unclean thing, and all our righteousnesses are like filthy rags; we all fade as a leaf, and our iniquities, like the wind, have taken us away (Isaiah 64:6)." The original Hebrew words translated 'filthy rags' refer to the cloths women used to absorb their menstrual flow.[2] Need I say more?

On top of our conscience, the culture at large constantly points out "what's wrong" with us and hounds us to hide our flaws. We try to comply because we want to be validated. In this social media culture we covet the "thumbs up" and the "like." *Maybe if I plaster on enough makeup and trim down to just the right size I'll be acceptable.* That's what we hope, but when we close our door, take off the makeup, gadgets, and gizmos and look at the woman in the mirror, what do we believe about her? Does she have value? What or who is it based on? Emily found herself wrestling with these questions.

> *Yes, I still find myself trying to cover my shortcomings. I attempt to hide them by avoiding whatever the situation [is]. Physically, I try to cover/hide whatever part of my body I'm not happy with so that others don't see. Emotionally, I put up a wall and [do] not allow people to get close to me. It takes vulnerability [on] my behalf to feel comfortable enough to put my emotions out there. That doesn't happen quickly for me. I have to gain trust in the person that I'm exposing myself to in that manner.*

Emily, like so many of us, wears different masks to cover the areas where she doesn't measure up. Whether it's to appear "pulled together" or to avoid ridicule, it all boils down to the same thing—hiding our shame. Don't be fooled, though, celebrities don't have it any better!

They hit that red carpet putting faith in stylists and designers that they'll step out looking flawless. At least for that night, the public will care less about their latest failed marriage or embarrassment in the tabloids. It's all about how flawless and fabulous they appear at the moment, but it's only temporary.

The makeup melts off at the end of the night; the gown and jewels go back the next day. They're back to the reality they see in the mirror. Then there's the pressure of having to top that look next awards' show because the public is so hard to please. Many celebrities live for those moments even though the outfits have no transformative power in their lives and don't give their lives meaning.

So what's the alternative? Where do we find relief from the constant message that we don't meet the world's arbitrary standards, much less God's? Where do we find approval and validation? Who is it based on? Again we look to the cross of Christ because of the value He ascribed to us there.

Notice I said value, not worth. Do you love a good deal? I certainly do. When I part with my money I need to know what I'm getting in exchange is worth the cost. The real rush is buying something that's costly to manufacture, at a deep discount. That's the way of this world isn't? An investment's worth depends on the volume of demand.

At face value, DADDY God got the short end of the deal. No offense, but we are not in high demand and we're certainly no bargain! Christ's life for yours or mine *definitely* wasn't a worthy, or equal, exchange. Yet DADDY God sees us in ways we don't see ourselves or each other! We are precious to Him, of prized importance. So much so, He laid His perfect Son's life down, with Jesus in full agreement, so we could be made right.

> For He [the Father] made Him [Jesus] who knew no sin to be sin for us, that we might become the righteousness of God in Him [Jesus]. — 2 Corinthians 5:21, emphasis mine

Jesus is awesome! He literally took on all of our sin and imperfection, every way we fall short of God's glory. Then He received all of the guilt, shame and judgment our sin deserved so that we could receive the righteousness and perfect standing in DADDY God's eyes that we don't deserve! It will take the rest of eternity to wrap our minds around that so DADDY God gave us a visual, spelled out in terms us girls could understand...a wardrobe change!

We've been given a gorgeous garment that requires no shapewear and looks fabulous on any frame. It's a dazzling robe, so bright it's white in appearance and freely given to every DADDY's girl. This robe is not about smoke and mirrors. Its brilliance isn't designed to distract an onlooker's attention from judging you. The robe's not masking anything; it's *highlighting* the perfection of your clothier, Jesus.

> I will greatly rejoice in the Lord,
> My soul shall be joyful in my God;
> For He has clothed me with the
> garments of salvation, He has

covered me with the <u>robe of
righteousness</u>, As a bridegroom
decks himself with ornaments,
And as a bride adorns herself with
her jewels. — Isaiah 61:10,
emphasis mine

For most women, there is no more important event
for which she pulls out all the stops than her wedding
day. From the dress, to the shoes, to the hair, veil and
jewels, a bride is an absolute vision! This robe of
righteousness is likened to the abundance of radiant
jewels covering a Middle Eastern bride. If you're a
DADDY's girl, that's Christ Jesus' robe you're
wearing. Just like a bride's dazzling jewels beautifully
finishes her bridal ensemble, Jesus' righteousness
takes us beyond being pleasing to God to perfection in
His eyes! It's Jesus' righteousness, or right standing,
with DADDY God given to us because Jesus paid, in
full, our sin in our place (see 2 Corinthians 5:21). He's
the only one who could have paid it; thank God He
was willing!

Though readily available, this robe of righteousness isn't selected by everyone, and rightly so, if one's chief concern is denial and concealment It's human nature to try to hide the things that condemn us, that bring judgment from others.

Try as we might, we can't hide from our conscience which knowing our guilt, demands justice. Yet the only One who could condemn us, instead took those very flaws and nailed them to the cross, judging them there (see Colossians 2:13-14). The guilty stain removed and forgotten forever, our conscience is soothed.

The robe of righteousness is only for those who've taken their place as Christ's bride, acknowledging He paid for our sin in our place. One has to submit to Jesus' cleansing by His blood, having given up all efforts to look just right, before sporting something so permanent because it is revealing. Not your shame, certainly not. That's been dealt with at the cross already. Jesus judged those things you're ashamed of, worthless, compared to the value He sees in you (see Hebrews 12:2). No, this robe reveals your perfection as one washed and kept clean by Jesus' perfect blood!

> But if we walk in the light as He is
> in the light, we have fellowship
> with one another, and the blood of
> Jesus Christ His Son cleanses us
> from all sin. —1 John 1:7

What to believe, then, when dull roars within and without cry 'failure' and 'hypocrite' (yes, I hear them too). BELIEVE! Believe you, received as is and made new, are now expertly fitted and adorned in Jesus' righteousness. You didn't earn it, because you couldn't. You can't do anything to maintain it either. N O O N E C A N . Your righteousness is a gift, not a reward. More than acceptance, it's absolute approval. A statement piece declaring DADDY God finds **no fault in you**.

> [He exclaimed] O my love, how
> beautiful you are! There is no
> flaw in you! — Song of Solomon
> 4:7, AMP

Do yourself a favor and read that verse again. These are the words of the bridegroom to his bride, representing Jesus Christ and His bride, the Church (see Ephesians 5:25). Did you see the words "no flaw in you?" Do you see the exclamation points? This isn't mumbled, but passionately declared! "How could it be?" you ask. It's only by grace through faith, girlfriend. Faith that all that's right about Jesus was more than enough to pay for all that's wrong with you and me.

Jesus is your righteousness and mine. There is no other righteousness. He alone is your stamp of approval because He laid it all on the line to declare your value. Our standing in Him never changes; neither does DADDY God's good opinion of us. He sees us as **a** finished work, because of **THE** finished work.

Let's not look inward or outward at all the things that trip us up. Instead let's let the Holy Spirit work out our underlying issues and look upward to Jesus exalted and all that's right about Him (see Hebrews 12:1-2). By faith in Christ, we wear His perfect righteousness, though in our daily experience we're undergoing remodeling. I encourage you to believe in His work and take Him at His word.

> But this Man [Christ Jesus], after He had offered one sacrifice for sins forever, sat down at the right hand of God... For by one offering He has <u>perfected forever</u> those who are <u>being sanctified</u>. — Hebrews 10: 12, 14, emphasis mine

In Christ's robe we can come boldly before DADDY God. Not because we've done right but because **Jesus did right** on the cross. In His robe we can cast our cares on DADDY God because He cares for us (see 1 Peter 5:7). In His robe we're refused no good thing because our faith brings DADDY God pleasure (see Psalm 84:11). We wear the robe of righteousness, the robe of the Beloved, full of grace and truth (see John 1:14). We wear it to the glory of our DADDY God.

> Therefore, since we have been made right in God's sight by faith, we have peace with God because of what Jesus Christ our Lord has done for us. Because of our faith, Christ has brought us into this place of highest privilege where we now stand, and we confidently and joyfully look forward to sharing God's glory. — Romans 5:1-2, NLT

Rejoice, relax, you are all right with God. At the beginning and end of the day when you look in the mirror free of all earthly adornment, don't see yourself bare, flaws glaring. Reality is about how DADDY God sees you, beautiful and flawless, courtesy of Christ. Robed in His righteousness, you are as clean inside as the robe is glorious. Smile at the woman you see looking back! Jesus is her righteousness and her Righteousness is forever!

"I'm a real woman who shines brightest when lifted on Jesus' shoulders."

SIX

Suffering in Silence

As a little girl, what woman, real or fictional, made you feel capable and strong? I'd have to say, Wonder Woman. I had the costume and the undies and when I wore them, you couldn't tell me I was weak! The truth is, though, I was and still am, because my abilities are limited. It's taken me a while to embrace that as reality rather than a fault to overcome.

However, I must say, you and I *are* quite capable. It's amazing how many hats women wear and what we accomplish every day. If we're honest, though, we'll admit we're not self-sufficient, and neither are men! We were all created to do life in the company of others, ultimately dependent on our God. Since we need our DADDY God, He gave us Jesus. Not only is He the only way to a relationship with DADDY God, He's the full manifestation of His Father.

Jesus Himself says, "Anyone who has seen me has seen the Father (John 14:9, NIV)." In Jesus we have life: abundant, victorious, and complete. He is our supply, even more than we could ever need.

"Yeah but I can do anything I set my mind to, Vanessa, and I tell my daughter she can do the same!" I hear you. My daughter and I are each other's biggest cheerleaders, but let's put it in the proper context.

> I can do all things <u>through Christ</u>
> who strengthens me. —Philippians
> 4:13, emphasis mine

I'm all about "girl power" and dreaming big, but the reality is human beings have limitations. We don't know and can't do everything. Christ is our inexhaustible supply. We can do whatever He empowers us to do.

That's completely contrary to the messages we hear every day. In this world, respect is given proportionate to your productivity and stamina. How much can be put on your plate and you still perform? Women have even greater pressure to prove our abilities, especially in the workforce.

Single women may find the grind more tolerable, being pulled in relatively fewer directions. Yet, for single mothers and those married with children, the stress is larger scale since most mothers in the workforce are still the primary caregivers of their children. We can't be everywhere at once *or* be all things to all people, yet we put on our imaginary super hero costume every day and try to do both. We *try*.

As a 1st generation American, you could say I'm prewired with an air of determination. I watched my parents hustle and work hard for everything we enjoyed and I expected no less of myself. Thanks to them, I attended wonderful private schools where I graduated with top grades. I believed I had to work hard and as long as **I** did, **I**'d always come out on top. That belief in **my** "unlimited" ability was soon tested.

During my first year of college I realized there were holes in my superhero cape. I went to college out of state with nothing but my longstanding vision of a Pediatric practice, my parent's financial support, and high expectations (theirs and mine). The rest would be up to me. *I've worked hard before,* I thought, *how hard could it be?* I quickly found success didn't come as surely as it had in previous years. The adjustment from high school to college is a steep learning curve and the considerable effort I put into my studies didn't pay off as it had in the past.

I studied hard only to fail some exams, leaving me devastated and humbled. With my dad being a 'pull yourself up by your own bootstraps' kind of guy, I knew I had two options. Get it together quickly or transfer to a college close to home and give up the dream. Convinced transferring would be interpreted as failure and invite ridicule; I said nothing about my challenges and muddled through.

Silently muddling through was not a new concept. I'd done it for years trying to please a father who genuinely wanted more opportunities for me, which in his mind required academic perfection. How could I disappoint him? Pushing through was the only way I saw to earn the respect of a man who had to fend for himself since age 15.

By my second year of college I'd given my life to Christ, the only One who could quench my thirst for unconditional love and compassion. My childhood dream weighed heavy on me at times as a career in medicine is no easy pursuit! My natural drive stressed me enough without tying parental expectation to it. I needed DADDY God's help; my strength wasn't enough. He gave me the Savior, His Son, mighty in compassion *and* strength.

> Therefore I take pleasure in infirmities, in reproaches, in needs, in persecutions, in distresses, for Christ's sake. For when I am weak, then I am strong.
> — 2 Corinthians 12:10

Here's my reality check: I'm not a superhero. DADDY God never told me to be one. He never told me to suffer in silence either. I'm a real woman who shines brightest when lifted on Jesus' shoulders. There is no shame in my weaknesses as they're opportunities to show who Jesus is, my glorious Savior. My weaknesses let Him be Lord; displaying what a loving God does for and through His beloved people.

Jesus promised to meet me in the valleys, the places of struggle and loneliness, not just give begrudging approval when I finally clawed my way to the mountain top. Like His DADDY, Jesus is faithful and I can testify of His goodness! He is the only reason I made it through those swirling, chest deep waters, constantly threatening to take me under. He took my hand and miraculously saw me through college, medical school, and two residencies.

I did the pediatric residency near the NYC borough where I first imagined the possibility. The preventive medicine residency came about because I wanted to have a broader scale impact, at the policy level, on children's health and welfare. I had never heard of the field until halfway through the pediatric residency, but Jesus opened doors and gave me favor with the program director That decade was a tremendous faith walk in Christ!

That season taught me something I'm constantly reminded of: put no confidence in the flesh or human effort (see Philippians 3:3). If I can wade through, I'll try to manage things on my own, ignoring my Savior's outstretched hand. "Oh what needless pain we bear all because we do not carry everything to God in prayer." DADDY God wants you and me to know He didn't just send Jesus to save us from hell, but to save us from ourselves, our hurts, and our misguided beliefs. I believed that since no one gave me compassion or encouragement, I was alone to fend for myself. I put on a fake cape with no power, depending on myself, until my flesh (self-effort) failed me as well.

Remember Regina, the woman totally abandoned by her father? She also struggles with a hesitance to ask for help, preferring to rely on herself. In fact, the only reason her story appears in this book is because she appreciated how difficult it was *for me* to ask for contributors!

Most times I will just go without before asking for help... I would say that most of the time I am a 'do it myself' kind of woman. I've been 'doing it myself' for some time. I guess this way of life happened at the age of 14 (when my mom got sick). I've been working since then and haven't stopped. For a long time, I've just depended on myself to make things happen. I will work myself until I'm half dead before asking for help. I fear hearing the word 'NO' or 'I can't' from others. I seek out help so seldom that I just can't fathom or understand why I would be turned down.

Her last sentence really resonates with me. "I seek out help so seldom that I just can't fathom or understand why I would be turned down." Being that we're both slow to ask for help, it stands to reason we'd only ask people we believe *would* help. She doesn't say how she interprets the 'no' in response to her infrequent requests for help, but in my experiences I've seen it as a value statement. "You're not that important to me; you don't rate as high as you thought," leaving me to the conclusion I should have just handled it myself. That's the same conclusion self-proclaimed independent woman, Emily, came to.

> *Yes, I am a "do it yourself," independent woman. I am like that because of all the disappointment I've had from people in my life. I feel like it is best to just depend on myself and not worry about getting disappointed [by] depending on someone else. It takes a lot for me to ask for help. If I do ask for help and I don't get the response or help that I expect, I feel like I should have just done it myself.*

This silent suffering seems to be a learned behavior of several women, typically after years of disappointment. That's how Sheila ended up "fending for herself" after several empty promises from the men in her childhood. She lived in survival mode for some time, but since coming into relationship with Christ, is learning that God wants her to thrive. "It's a process, but the growth and healing I'm experiencing has been worth it."

People typically make time for whom and what's important to them. With the world's current preoccupation with busyness, priority lists become shorter and shorter. What do you do if you don't "rate" as high with a loved one or friend as you once thought? Typically, we avoid the awkward 'sorry I can't' by putting more on our own plates, only to be let down by our own limits.

I'm so thankful for Jesus. Not only does He care, He always has time for me, and He's delighted to save the day! I especially love when He makes room in someone's heart for me. More than ever, I appreciate those who make time to listen and actually care. In all likelihood they pushed some things aside to do it.

Recently I heard a young woman's beautiful testimony regarding her unborn child. Several months pregnant, she received a call from her obstetrician stating her unborn son had a fatal genetic disease with a dim prognosis. Once born, he'd likely only have hours to live, a year at best.

Devastated and sobbing she tried several times to contact her husband. When she couldn't reach him she called her dad, since he and her husband worked together. Hearing her distress, her father pressed her to tell him the problem.

When she shared the doctor's report, he emphatically replied, "It's not true, that's a lie. Don't receive it. Your son is healthy." After gathering the rest of the family, he led them in prayer and reminded them of God's promises. Understandably, she continued to cry and worry about her son, but eventually her trust in God swelled as they stood on His Word.

When she and her husband met with the specialist days later for further testing, they were told their son is healthy and developing well! He didn't find any evidence of the previously diagnosed genetic disease! In tears, she told the congregation she couldn't ask for a more supportive family.

Did you notice it all started with a father who supplied strength in his daughter's moment of weakness? Life dealt his daughter a blow and he was there. She wasn't even looking for him, but she needed to hear from her daddy. She needed to hear him speak words of spirit and life with the authority of a shepherd (see John 6:63).

His affirmation, love, and leadership were priceless. He shouldered her burden by gathering the entire family and leading them in prayer. Recognizing her weakness in that moment, he encouraged her to latch on to his faith and turned her attention to her DADDY God; the One who could turn the situation around.

> Now to Him who is able to do exceedingly abundantly above all that we ask or think, according to the power that works in us, to Him be glory in the church by Christ Jesus to all generations, forever and ever. Amen.
> — Ephesians 3:20-21

In this instance, her daddy represented DADDY God well as His ambassador. As any good ambassador, he knew his limits. His daughter's faith didn't belong in him, but in the faithfulness of the One he represents.

I cried when I heard that testimony. I cried as a mother imagining the horrible experience, and thankful I've never known it. I cried in joy at the glory given to God, and the loving leadership of a father who played a tremendous part in that. I did not cry in envy and self-pity, though.

I rejoiced for her even though that father-daughter exchange is not my reality. My dad doesn't encourage me in that way, but my DADDY God is quick to help when I'm caught in life's undertow! DADDY God provided a Savior who's with me in the rising tides of life and speaks peace to raging storms.

> When you pass through the waters, I will be with you, and through the rivers, they will not overwhelm you. When you walk through the fire, you will not be

burned or scorched, nor will the
flame kindle upon you...I, even I,
am the Lord, and besides Me there
is no Savior.

— Isaiah 43:2, 11, AMP

I'm not left to suffer in silence, carrying my
burdens alone. Jesus is with me. He is DADDY God's
abundant supply of help in time of need (see Hebrews
4:16). He both steadies and strengthens me. Storms
cease at His word. When I rest in Jesus, His Word and
His finished work, I'm weightless, able to ride above
what threatens to take me under. My DADDY made
sure of it.

Wouldn't you like to enjoy that rest? You can.

SEVEN

Go Ahead, Lean on Him

You know what? It's only now as a woman, wife, and mother of three extraordinary children that I'm *coming* to the end of myself (it's a journey). By that I mean increasingly less dependence on my wisdom and determination to overcome challenges. Life is a beautiful and humbling enterprise, and all the more with each ball added to my juggling routine.

It's much easier to feel overwhelmed by life now than it did as a single medical student and resident physician. Marathon study sessions and sleepless nights on-call pale in comparison to my current 24/7/365 reality. Daily, I'm pulled in a myriad of directions and that's just as wife and mother of three uniquely strong-willed children, not to mention home manager, writer, etc.

It doesn't matter if you're single, married with children, or somewhere in between; if you have breath in your body there are people placing demands on you (your time, attention, talent, resources, etc). YOU may be the most demanding of yourself!

Some of the demands on you are warranted, some aren't, but you're not designed to meet any of them in your own strength. So don't. Your strength and wisdom are finite and faulty. DADDY God in His mercy beckons us to trust in His supply, Jesus. Rest in Him and lean on Him.

> Trust in the LORD with <u>all</u> your heart and lean not on your own understanding; in <u>all</u> your ways

> acknowledge him, and he will
> make your paths straight. —
> Proverbs 3.5-6 NIV, emphasis
> mine

From early on in my walk with Jesus these became, and remain, my favorite verses of Scripture. I guess they resonated with me because I'm so prone to self-reliance and these verses DO NOT allow for that. I can't trust **in** my effort, abilities, ideas, and solutions at all, if ALL my trust is in Jesus and His direction. Not only is His perspective and understanding perfect, His execution of a matter is flawless (see Psalm 18:30). Trusting in Him is a win-win every time!

However, if you're stubborn like me, there's nothing like life's complexities to bring you around to His way of thinking. How many times, in knee-jerk response, have you followed what seems a perfectly reasonable plan only to realize it wasn't best? What about complete exhaustion from over commitment relative to the number of hours in a day? Several military moves with, now, three children, whom I home-educated at one point, brought this high-achiever to the realization I talked about in the last chapter. I AM NOT WONDER WOMAN.

I can't do it all, not in my own strength. Honestly I don't do anything in my own strength because all I am and all I do are by the grace of God. Able as we may appear, we're still mere mortals with faults and weaknesses.

"Wait a minute, Vanessa. Shouldn't we do our best?" Of course! When we do something out of the abundance we've received, we'll inevitably do our best. However, doing our best and believing an outcome is completely dependent on our effort are two different things. If we keep gritting our teeth and grinding through, we'll only ruin ourselves. We're not on this earth left to fend for ourselves like abandoned orphans. We have a DADDY who draws near, not to demand, but to give of Himself.

> For thus says the Lord God, the
> Holy One of Israel: "In returning
> and rest you shall be saved; in
> quietness and confidence shall be

> your strength." But you would
> not... — Isaiah 30:15

God said these words to the children of Israel, who had a penchant for depending on their strength and those of other nations. Through the prophet Isaiah, the Lord goes on to say He's waiting to show them grace, if they would only allow Him. They were striving and hustling to accomplish what God wanted to **give them**. They sought answers both from within and those around them, but they forgot to look up.

God offered them rest, peace, true confidence and strength. They only had to return to the reality of their complete dependence on Him. They would not. Will you? There are many reasons Jesus died on a cross, elevated above the ground. What if one of them was to remind us to look up for our every need (see Psalm 121:1)?

At the cross, Jesus ushered in the new covenant, the covenant of grace (God's goodness to the undeserving). None of us deserve God's goodness, so we all qualify for God's grace! The key to receiving grace is admitting you need it. That means admitting you 'don't know—,' 'don't have—,' or 'can't do—' and then confidently asking Him for the wisdom, provision, strength, or whatever else you may need. It means freely acknowledging when you've made a mess; because you know He gives grace to the humble (see James 4:6). Remember the prodigals we met in chapter 1? They thought they'd gone too far to find their way back home, only to find an open door and open arms upon arrival!

Receiving grace also means pausing before implementing your bright idea to ask Him what's best. It's resting in DADDY's love for you and Christ's work of salvation and the deliverance it brings. It's abiding in His peace, not because all is well around you, but because He's holding you. And because DADDY God's thoughts of and plans for you are always good, you confidently expect good (see Jeremiah 29:11). That, my friend, is strength! Real strength is depending on His, rather than ours.

> "Come to Me, all you who labor
> and are heavy laden, and I will
> give you rest. Take My yoke upon

> you and learn from Me, for I am
> gentle and lowly in heart, and you
> will find rest for your souls. For
> My yoke is easy and My burden is
> light." — Matthew 11:28-30,
> emphasis mine

Jesus says it best. If you're weary from toiling under demands placed on you, come to Him; He will cause you to rest. It may be hard to notice Him calling when you're busy trying to meet a self-imposed standard, or when those closest to you see your load, but don't or won't help. Just know your DADDY God sees you and He sent you a Savior.

You're not supposed to have all the answers, fix all the problems, or tough it out on your own. Change your belief from "work to be worthy" to "rest to receive." Jesus is near and He's an extravagant giver just like His DADDY!

Have you read about the unnamed woman in the book of Luke who was crippled for 18 years (see Luke 13:10-17)? A demonic spirit wore her down till she was bent over, her eyes fixed on the ground. Many of us are like this "daughter of Abraham" in that we're weighed down under the burden of demands and the guilt in not being able to meet all of them.

We don't know exactly how her condition developed, but we know it came from the pit of hell and kept her stuck for 18 years. Clearly she tried to straighten herself up because the text tells us she was unable to. All she was aware of, day in and day out were the circumstances down around her. She could never look up, have another perspective.

Jesus saw her in the synagogue and called her over to declare her "loosed from the spirit of infirmity." Laying hands on her, she immediately became straight, having a perspective found only by looking into Jesus's eyes. Then she could see hope and grace, a supply greater than what's down around her!

Do you have a spirit of infirmity? Thoughts or emotions that weigh you down, habits you can't break, demands you can't satisfy. Are you bent over in discouragement and weariness? One thing is certain, if you're carrying a burdensome load, Jesus didn't give it to you. He's in the business of loosing and lifting.

He wants you to swap that weight for His light and easy yoke.

While Jesus carries the load, we walk with Him, learning about Him, and following His lead. Since He isn't demanding, our souls recover and rest in His presence. Go ahead, *lean* on Him. He's not like people, well-meaning but incapable, or bound by their own issues. He sees your heaviness and says, "Come, let me relieve you of that cumbersome burden."

Do you believe He will do it? That woman burdened and bent over came when Jesus called her because she believed He was both willing and able to do something about her condition. He did more than *something*, He changed her life!

Life in Christ is lived by faith (see Romans 1:17). Faith, simply defined, is complete dependence on Jesus' finished work at the cross. There He accomplished what David spoke of in Psalm 138:8; He perfected (completed) those things which concern us. Whether those concerns are personal, family issues or demands at work, our best response is from a place of rest and confidence in what Jesus has done.

> There remains, then, a Sabbath-
> rest for the people of God; for
> anyone who enters God's rest also
> rests from his own work, just as
> God did from his. Let us,
> therefore, make every effort to
> enter that rest, so that no one will
> fall by following their example of
> disobedience.
>
> — Hebrews 4:9-11, NIV

DADDY God wants us to live life in Sabbath rest; Spirit-led, not harried. Here's a newsflash: 'woman' is not defined as a female running around like a headless chicken! If there's anything we should be in a hurry to do, it's to *draw* on Jesus before we *do* anything.

Most women experience some degree of what I call the "Mary-Martha tension" within them. At the end of chapter 10 of Luke's gospel account we discover how differently these two sisters see Jesus. Having welcomed Him into their home, Martha immediately got **busy** preparing a meal for Him. A natural doer, she perceived a need to be met, though Jesus didn't ask her for food.

Tense and flustered, by her self-imposed burden, she noticed her sister listening restfully at Jesus' feet and took offense. *How could He chatter on with Mary while I'm working tirelessly for Him?!* She didn't just think it, she said as much to Him—and so have I. With gentleness and tact, Jesus assured Martha that Mary's perspective was the better of the two. Mary perceived her own need and saw Jesus as THE supply. She didn't see her neediness as something to be hidden, not in the presence of unceasing supply. She chose to fill up on Him before *doing* anything.

The world would have us all be permanent Martha's, reacting immediately, running to and fro. DADDY God's way is facing life after fully satisfying ourselves with the Holy Spirit's revelation of Jesus in the Word. Mary rested at Jesus' feet listening to His every word. There is nothing more important actually, but here is the tension. We all juggle several balls in the air—family, career, church, and friends. Things do need to get done. Shouldn't Mary get up and help fix a meal? Everybody needs to eat at some point! Yes, we all have responsibilities, but Jesus advises quieting ourselves in His presence and listening to Him *first.*

It reminds me of a personal mountain I faced recently, minor weight loss. Weight loss was the one topic you were anxiously waiting for me to bring up, wasn't it? I'm happy to oblige! All jokes aside, let me start by admitting I am not the poster child for diet and exercise. I always hoped I would never need to work out because it's never been my thing. Besides, a naturally fast metabolism served my small frame nicely my first 35 years. Things changed, though, after my 3rd child. My body didn't bounce back as fast, but the thought of long workouts and dieting repulsed me (I'm chocolate's biggest fan).

After sweating for months on my husband's treadmill and eating smaller portions resulted in nothing but frustration, I decided to bring it to Jesus. I told Him how heavy those extra 12 pounds felt and how poorly my clothes fit. Getting winded from just running up a flight of stairs irritated me. I needed to get rid of the weight so I asked Jesus for insight. His instructions were quite simple. After all, He knows my body best so He could zero in on the problem.

"Wait a minute, Vanessa! Why would you bother Him over losing 12 pounds? Didn't you have a bigger issue worthy of His time?" There was a time I thought I should only pray about "big concerns," but I've wised up. I bring all of it to Him! I figure if my DADDY bothers to know the number of hairs on my head (see Luke 12:7), He clearly cares about the "little things." I may as well let Jesus be "Lord of all" in my life.

As for my weight concerns, Jesus reminded me how much He and DADDY God loved me at that moment, at that size. He dealt with the root of my weight retention. I'd been feeling vulnerable which led to a fear of gaining weight, the very thing that came to pass!

> There is no fear in love; but perfect love casts out fear, because fear involves torment. But he who fears has not been made perfect in love. — 1 John 4:18

Assured of His love, the fear removed, He told me a couple of things to add to my diet and reminded me of the collection of quick dance workouts I already owned (much for more fun than running on a rotating belt).

Wouldn't you know, after yoking myself to His instruction, I lost the 12 pounds in 2 months that I couldn't shake for 2 years! To this day I maintain my weight by continuing in His instruction. I share this to say, walking with Jesus is as much practical as spiritual. You can bring anything to Him that bothers you or weighs you down (pun intended). He is the answer! I could've kept plugging away for years trying different workouts or diets plans with little progress; but why work harder when you can work wiser?

I encourage you to take Jesus up on His offer and yoke yourself to Him. He is the grace of DADDY God given to the undeserving and needy. Not just so we can go to heaven one day, but so we can have life beyond measure today!

The thief does not come except to steal, and to kill, and to destroy. I have come that they may have life, and that they may have it more abundantly. — John 10:10

Bring your cares to Him and follow His lead. He'll show you the way and how to make the most of the time and gifting DADDY God's given you. When Jesus stretched His arms wide on that cross, He not only received our sin and judgment. He hinted at His post-cross posture of supply, encouraging us to freely take what He freely gives (see 1 Corinthians 2:12). Even while ascending into heaven His nail pierced hands were extended, blessing His disciples (see Luke 24:50-51).

Jesus has DADDY God's heart. He wants you successful in every area and the shortest distance between two points is still a straight line. As you lean on Jesus, He leads you on straight paths of good success (see Joshua 1:8). Holy Spirit, help us be women of prayer, meditating on the Word of Christ, and resting in His finished work. Amen.

"...for He [God] Himself has said, I will not in any way fail you nor give you up nor leave you without support." — Hebrews 13:5a, AMP

Between Us Girls...

We've covered a lot of ground, haven't we? Between us girls we've looked at numerous Scriptures confronting negative beliefs about DADDY God. We've seen the connection between those beliefs and negative father/daughter relationships through the stories shared by women, just like you and me.

They, like us, are on a life long journey: discovering what it means to be DADDY's girls, to trust Him wholeheartedly. Entrusting their lives to Jesus was the first, and necessary, step. Why did they risk disappointment and surrender their lives to Jesus Christ?

Regina —

I gave my life to Christ because I was tired of feeling empty inside! In the past, I tried everything imaginable to fill the gaping hole inside me. I spent many years of my life reaching out to my dad and longing for his love, but I got little or no love in return. For many years, I sought happiness in partying, smoking, and drinking, but felt depressed, miserable, and empty at the end of the day. I gave my life to Christ because I needed my tank, my soul filled! What I was doing and the people I sought to fill me up weren't working.

Sheila —

With so many feelings of abandonment, I knew my life was missing something

...somebody. I yearned for someone to protect me, but in the physical. I'm not sure that anyone could heal my internal pain. In spite of my multiple thoughts of suicide, putting myself in risky situations, and so many close calls, I knew that it must have been God who spared me. He was the Father who protected me and I knew I couldn't live my life without Him. As I studied His Word, prayed, and got connected with other believers, the void in my heart grew smaller.

Danielle —

Starting from the age of 4 until age 8, my only example of a man was my biological father. I have some great memories and some bad memories. I've witnessed my father emotionally and physically mistreat my mother. However, I know God had his hand on *her life because her only response was prayer, smiles and unconditional love. When my parents divorced, I was asked, "Which parent do you want to live with?" My mom sat me down and explained that no matter what I decided she would always love me and God would protect me. My decision was clear. I trusted God and stayed with my mother. I made the decision in my heart, mind, and soul to choose God.*

Emily —

I grew up in the church and have always been exposed to the Word of God. Growing up, I would often question why God allowed me to have a birth father that physically and emotionally abused me. When I was 6 years old, my aunt married a man that became a father figure in my life. He played a major role in my life until he was tragically killed in a work related accident when I was 16 years old. I was devastated by his death and I began to question God again about why He would do this to me. I just didn't understand. Over time, He revealed to me that He was my father and that I needed to depend on Him in all aspects of my life. Trusting was a hard concept for me because every time I got to a place of trusting someone, I would get disappointed. I knew God's voice and saw what He was capable of doing throughout my life, but I just thought it was for others and not for me. It wasn't until I gave my life to Christ that I started to see a shift in my life, in spite of major challenges since then. I know He's the only way I've been able to endure and continue through life's journey.

Every day these women spend with Jesus He's revealing more of His DADDY's heart to them, because Jesus only does what He sees His Father doing (see John 5:19, NIV). Therefore, to know Jesus *is* to know DADDY God, as well (see John 14:9). During our time together we've been discovering DADDY's heart toward us, demonstrated through all that Jesus has accomplished for us.

I hope, by now, you'll agree there's nothing like being a DADDY's girl. Our DADDY is good and He is good to us! His heart is full, not of judgment or criticism, but acceptance and delight — all because of Jesus.

You may find all we've learned about His goodness overwhelming. It may have challenged everything you've previously believed about God the Father. That's to be expected, so there is no need for anxiety or guilt over lingering thoughts of doubt, anger or resentment toward Him. In Christ, there is **nothing** that can condemn you or bring judgment against you in DADDY God's eyes (see Romans 8:1).

So you know what? You can relax. There are no hoops to jump through, no check lists of requirements to meet, and nothing to prove. You and I can rest, right now, confident our DADDY enjoys us. He's enjoying the woman you present to the world and the girl deep down inside. Remember, it's not your thoughts or actions that make you right with DADDY God; it's your position in Christ Jesus. Jesus is your righteousness!

What Jesus did for us can never be undone, not even by our inconsistencies. Your righteousness — that perfect standing you have in your DADDY's eyes — is a gift paid for with Jesus' blood. You didn't do anything to earn it so you can't do anything to lose it. In your DADDY's eyes you are **FAR** from who you used to be --- "you're **forgiven** forever, **accepted** in the Beloved and you are the **righteousness** of God in Christ."

For those of us who have countless layers of self-protective armor built up over many years, this truth must penetrate before it sinks down in our hearts. That will take time. It takes time to change the recording you've played in your mind for so long. To believe you ARE loved unconditionally and that DADDY God loves lavishing you with His grace. It takes time to go from pointing to achievements to establish your worth, to pointing to Jesus' finished work on the cross to affirm your value.

Make an event of the journey. Enjoy the process and celebrate the small break-throughs. Writing this book has been an amazing part of my own journey. I'm more aware of DADDY God's love for me today than before I started writing it, and it's changing how I see myself and relate to others. I certainly haven't "arrived," but I'm **FAR** from where I used to be!

If this book has blessed you, I encourage you to read it often. Look up the Scriptures I've referenced and memorize as many as speak to your heart. Then meditate on every word in those verses. Meditating is just talking about the meaning of each word in a verse, but it makes all the difference. It takes you from just knowing the words of a verse to believing them with all your heart. Meditating on Scriptures full of love, grace, and the beauty of the Jesus' finished work build trust in DADDY God and His unfailing love for us.

One more thing, there's nothing like reading God's word and doing life in the company of other believers. I encourage you to find a church that preaches Jesus and the gracious gospel He came to give us. As you dive into the Word, with the support of your church family, you'll discover all you are and have in Christ.

While you make yourself at home in DADDY God's heart, I pray you experience the expansive dimensions of His love expressed in Christ. May you enjoy rest, peace and joy in your DADDY's arms forever! There's nothing like being a DADDY's girl!

NOTES

Can We Talk...
1. The Names of God. *Preceptaustin*. Retrieved in 2015 from http://www.preceptaustin.org/abba-father.htm.

Come Home
1. Greek Lexicon :: G5485 (KJV). Retrieved in 2015 from http://www.blueletterbible.org/lang/lexicon/lexicon.cfm?Str ongs=G5485&t=KJV

Fathers and Daughters
1. Hebrew Lexicon :: H622 (KJV). Retrieved in 2015 from http://www.blueletterbible.org/lang/Lexicon/Lexicon.cfm?S trongs=H622&t=KJV

Flawless!
1. O'Connor, Clare. (2012, March 26). *Undercover Billionaire: Sara Blakely Joins The Rich List Thanks To Spanx*. Retrieved from http://www.forbes.com/sites/clareoconnor/2012/03/07/unde rcover-billionaire-sara-blakely-joins-the-rich-list-thanks-to-spanx/#2715e4857a0b111da5f2427e

2. Hebrew Lexicon :: H5708 (KJV). Retrieved in 2015 from http://www.blueletterbible.org/lang/lexicon/lexicon.cfm?Str ongs=H5708&t=KJV

117

ACKNOWLEDGEMENTS

To my DADDY God and the Lord Jesus Christ: Your grand and loving plan made it possible for your girls to come home. Your love for us is overwhelming in the most beautiful way!

To my Dad: You're a great man who's always done the best you could, with what you were given. You've played a big part in the woman I've become. I'm thankful for you and I love you!

To my husband, Mark: Your unwavering love and support has helped turn me from caterpillar into butterfly! I fly higher when you cheer me on.

To Joshua, Andrew, and Hannah: Your love for me reminds me of DADDY God's: limitless and transformative. Thank you for believing the best about me!

To the contributing DADDY's Girls: Your courage and transparency are testament to your growing security in DADDY God's love for you. I'm blessed to call you friends. Thank you for sharing!

ABOUT VANESSA

VANESSA A. HARRIS, M.D., M.S. has been described as loyal, compassionate, and witty, which offsets her disarming candor. A proud, native New Yorker born to West Indian immigrants, she enjoyed growing up in the Bronx.

Vanessa's blogging and other writing projects are a big departure from the life of prescription writing and patient charting she envisioned. After completing Pediatric and Preventive Medicine residencies along with a Master of Science degree, she was all set to fulfill a childhood dream, at the public policy level. It was during this time she married her husband, an officer in the United States Coast Guard, and began a family.

Vanessa's "master plan" changed when the Lord called her to stay home and care for her own children full time. At her first Love's request and with her husband's support, Vanessa put her medical career aside to give her own children a firm foundation from which to approach the world. That difficult and unpopular sacrifice has since benefited her family greatly. Before and since becoming a military wife, Vanessa has lived all over the U.S. and has been privileged to acclimate her children to its various regions and cultures, even homeschooling them over a 3-year period.

A once avid journal writer, Vanessa became drawn to other writing outlets. Hoping to impact children's lives in a way policy never could, she began writing children's stories and blogging revelations about her parenting exploits with the Lord. She's also completed the Institute of Children's Literature's course on Writing for Children and Teenagers, as well as, other short courses on writing. Vanessa's passion is encouraging believers, especially mothers, to trust in

Jesus and His work, not our efforts. Today she writes the blog, *Vine Life Faith: Living by Grace through Faith*, where she shares posts on faith and family along with her poetry.

These days, Vanessa's organic writing journey takes place in Texas, where she's finally settled down with her husband, Mark Harris CDR, USCG (ret.), their children, and her NY edge.

STAY CONNECTED WITH VANESSA

CHECK OUT Vanessa's Kreativ Blogger awarded blog, *Vine Life Faith*, at www.vinelifefaith.com. Sign up for FREE resources, encouraging posts, and updates on upcoming books!

EMAIL her at vanessaharris@vinelifefaith.com

CHAT with her on Twitter @VanessaxGrace

29925827R00085

Made in the USA
Middletown, DE
07 March 2016